MAY   2012

DISCARD

.PL discards materials that are outdated
and in poor condition in order to make
room for current, in-demand materials.
Underused materials are offered for
public sale

CONTEMPORARY LIVES

KIM KARDASHIAN

REALITY TV STAR

ABDO
Publishing Company

CONTEMPORARY LIVES

KIM KARDASHIAN

REALITY TV STAR

by Joanne Mattern

CREDITS

Published by ABDO Publishing Company, PO Box 398166,
Minneapolis, MN 55439. Copyright © 2012 by Abdo Consulting
Group, Inc. International copyrights reserved in all countries.
No part of this book may be reproduced in any form without
written permission from the publisher. The Essential Library™ is a
trademark and logo of ABDO Publishing Company.

Printed in the United States of America,
North Mankato, Minnesota
112011
012012

 THIS BOOK CONTAINS AT LEAST 10% RECYCLED MATERIALS.

Editors: Lisa Owings and Lauren Coss
Copy Editor: Christina Black
Series design: Emily Love
Cover and interior production: Kelsey Oseid

Library of Congress Cataloging-in-Publication Data

Mattern, Joanne, 1963-
  Kim Kardashian : reality tv star / by Joanne Mattern.
     p. cm. -- (Contemporary lives)
  Includes bibliographical references and index.
  ISBN 978-1-61783-326-7
  1. Kardashian, Kim, 1980---Juvenile literature. 2. Television
personalities--United States--Biography--Juvenile literature. 3.
Celebrities--United States--Biography--Juvenile literature. I. Title.
  PN1992.4.K345M38 2012
  791.4502'8092--dc23
  [B]
                                        2011042993

TABLE OF CONTENTS

Keeping Up with the Kardashians made Kim Kardashian a household name in the world of pop culture.

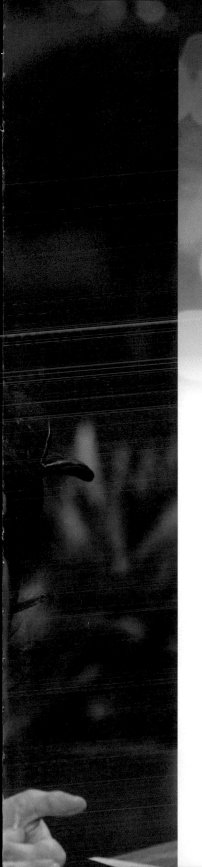

CHAPTER 1

TV's Newest Star

||||||||||||||||||||||||||

Who are the Kardashians? That's what people were wondering in October 2007 when the E! television network premiered its newest reality show, *Keeping Up with the Kardashians*. The show profiled Kim Kardashian and her family: sisters Khloe and Kourtney, brother Rob, mother Kris Jenner, stepfather Bruce Jenner, and half sisters Kylie and Kendall.

The family lived in a mansion in Calabasas, California, near Los Angeles. At the time, Kim, Khloe, and Kourtney owned the boutique Dash, which sold expensive clothing and accessories. Other than that, the only reason the family's name may have sounded familiar was the girls' late father, Robert Kardashian, had been a friend and attorney for O. J. Simpson during his highly publicized murder trial in the 1990s.

Kim Kardashian, however, was becoming famous for her own reasons. She was a good friend of Paris Hilton and Nicole Richie, two beautiful, rich, young women from celebrity families. Kardashian, Hilton, and Richie were often photographed going to clubs and restaurants. Kardashian was also getting attention because of her love life.

||||||||||||||||||||||||||||||||||||||||||||||||||||

ROMANCE, SCANDAL, AND FAME

"It started when I went out with Nick Lachey on a date," Kardashian recalled,

NICK LACHEY

||||||||||||||||||||||||||||||||||||||||||||||||||||||||||||||||||||||||||||||||||||||

Nick Lachey was a former member of the boy band 98 Degrees. In 2002, he married singer and actress Jessica Simpson. Their marriage was chronicled on the highly popular MTV reality series *Newlyweds*.

The couple divorced in 2005, but both Lachey and Simpson—and their romantic partners, such as Kim Kardashian—have remained popular material for the tabloids ever since.

We went out to the movies in the afternoon. It was one of the first dates he'd been on since splitting up with Jessica Simpson, or at least the first time he'd been on a date publicly. Of course the paparazzi took pictures, because people were curious about who he was with.[1]

In 2007, Kardashian began another high-profile relationship with rhythm and blues (R & B) singer Ray J. The media went into a frenzy after a video containing intimate content was leaked to the public. Kardashian was horrified to be famous for something that should have been kept private and she was not proud of. She tried to put the scandal behind her and get on with her life, but she could not escape the public's fascination with her.

|||||||||||||||||||||||||||||||||||||||||||||||||||

Kardashian's brief relationship with Ray J had lasting effects on her fame and reputation.

KEEPING UP WITH THE KARDASHIANS

It didn't take long for Kardashian's fame and notoriety to rub off on the rest of her family. The public soon got to know the whole Kardashian clan when the family got their own television show. Kathie Lee Gifford was one of the Kardashian family's closest friends and a popular talk-show host and entertainer, and she had encouraged the Kardashians to take their lives on television. Gifford was often at the Kardashians' home and was always entertained by the antics of the sisters and their parents. Kim wrote,

> Whenever Kathie Lee would visit us, she'd say, 'You are such a crazy family! Where are the

REALITY TELEVISION RULES THE AIRWAVES

Kim Kardashian is far from the first person to appear on her own reality television show. Reality programs have been around for a long time. As far back as 1948, host Allen Funt was delighting viewers with his show *Candid Camera*. That show used hidden cameras to catch the victims of practical jokes or other embarrassing situations.

Reality shows became more common during the late 1980s, when a strike by the Writers Guild of America meant new scripts could not be written. To provide programming that didn't need union writers, networks turned toward reality programs, which were also quick and cheap to produce.

One of the first modern reality series was *The Real World*, which began airing on MTV in 1992 and was still on as of 2011. The show's premise is simple: Eight strangers are chosen to live together in a house, and MTV's cameras film their interactions, conflicts, romances, and other drama. The show has been credited with starting the modern reality-television genre and has served as a model for many similar shows that have followed.

cameras? We need cameras in here!' She thought our family would make a really funny show.[2]

Kim and her family liked the idea. Kim's mother, Kris, reached out to another family friend, television and radio host Ryan Seacrest. Seacrest also thought a reality show featuring the Kardashians would be popular. He agreed to be the show's producer. Soon afterward, *Keeping Up with the Kardashians* began filming. It first aired on E! in October 2007.

RYAN SEACREST

Ryan Seacrest first became famous as the host of the hugely popular reality competition series *American Idol*. He soon became one of the hardest-working media personalities. Along with *American Idol*, Seacrest has hosted a daily radio show, a nightly news show on E!, and the weekly radio show *American Top 40*. He has produced several reality shows featuring the Kardashians and other reality stars and has hosted the annual *New Year's* *Rockin' Eve* live television special from Times Square in New York City every December 31.

Seacrest knows just being famous is not enough to carry a television show. Success "depends on the story. You can have somebody very famous and put cameras in their life, and it's just not interesting. I try to (find) the stories that are interesting to watch but are also relatable on universal levels," he said.[3]

Keeping Up with the Kardashians depicts the Kardashians' everyday lives, both personal and professional. Kim is regularly featured in the episodes, often shown overcoming an insecurity, such as her fear of speaking in public or her embarrassment at dancing in front of other people. The episodes regularly show Kim getting involved in new business ventures. However, Kim was not always the center of attention, and she didn't mind that one bit. Compared to her sisters, Kim considered herself to be boring and shy, and she knew the whole family would entertain viewers. Kim also wanted viewers to see that, despite living a lifestyle and having experiences most people never had, her family was loving and close and had the same values as many other US families.

Critics of *Keeping Up with the Kardashians* were dismissive of the storyline and annoyed at the Kardashians' efforts to promote themselves. One critic said, "There is something disturbing about the Kardashians' intense hunger for fame. But even worse—it is downright boring to watch this family live out their tedious lives."[4] *Variety*, an important industry publication, panned Kim as a noncelebrity and went on to say,

In keeping with the title, though, Keeping Up with the Kardashians *actually widens its lens to encompass the whole irritating brood—including Kim's sisters Khloe and Kourtney, mom-manager Kris, and stepdad Bruce Jenner . . .*[5]

However, not all viewers were interested in kicking the Kardashian family off their television screens. The show was an instant hit and was seen by a total of 1.3 million viewers each week. It was also the highest-rated Sunday night series among women aged 18 to 34.

Kim Kardashian was now a recognizable name, but *Keeping Up with the Kardashians* was only the beginning of her rise to fame. Over the next few

SCRIPTED?

Many reality shows are criticized for being scripted. Instead of the cameras recording events as they happen, most shows use re-creations of events or even set up confrontations and other incidents for the camera. Kardashian and her family are no exception. Although the Kardashians have not admitted it, many critics and even fans believe the Kardashians are acting out scenes from a script and not always going about their everyday lives. These critics have noticed that *Keeping Up with the Kardashians* often feels like a situation comedy, with made-up events that follow a script thought up by writers.

Kardashian and her mother were filmed playing bocce ball for an episode of *Keeping Up with the Kardashians*.

years, she would become one of the most famous and talked about young stars in the country.

||||||||||

From left to right, Kourtney, Kim, and Khloe filmed *Keeping Up with the Kardashians* in Southern California.

CHAPTER 2

Growing Up Kardashian

||||||||||||||||||||||||||||||||||||||||||||||||||||||||||||||||||||

Kimberly Noel Kardashian was born on October 21, 1980, in Los Angeles, California. Her father was businessman and attorney Robert Kardashian, and her mother was Kris Houghton Kardashian. Kris had worked as a flight attendant before marrying Robert. The two met at a racetrack and married after dating for four years. Just one year later, Kris gave birth to Kourtney, the oldest Kardashian child.

Kim followed a year later. Her sister Khloe was born four years after that, and brother Rob three years after Khloe.

The Kardashians lived in a big house in Beverly Hills. The girls called the house "Tower Lane" after the street it was located on and because the name made the house sound like something out of a fairy tale. The house did seem like it was from a storybook. It was located on a private road and had a long driveway leading to it. The property had a pool, a Jacuzzi, a pool house, a tennis court, and plenty of trees for privacy. In a book written by Kourtney, Kim, and Khloe, *Kardashian Konfidential*, the girls recall that their neighborhood was filled with celebrities. Rock-and-roll musician Bruce Springsteen lived next door to them, and comedian Jay Leno lived down the street.

The Kardashians were known for their lavish parties. The family threw barbecues for their friends and family almost every weekend. There were also dinner parties and events for grown-ups. However, the children were not left out of the fun. The family had an annual scavenger hunt on New Year's Eve. Kris also threw elaborate birthday parties for Kim and her sisters and brother. These

Kim was the Kardashians' second child.

parties usually included pony rides, petting zoos, clowns, or people dressed up as cartoon characters, such as Big Bird from *Sesame Street*.

A CLOSE-KNIT FAMILY

Kim, her siblings, and her parents were all very close. Kris and Robert always made sure to put their family first. The Kardashians ate dinner together every night, and they were expected to

Robert Kardashian, *center*, was active in the lives of his children, *from left*, Rob, Kim, Kourtney, and Khloe.

communicate with each other, not talk on the phone or watch television while they ate. Kim and her sisters were asked for their opinions and encouraged to speak their minds. Kim credits this with helping her and her sisters grow up to be confident women who expect to be taken seriously.

Robert Kardashian was very involved in his children's lives. He always made sure they had finished their homework, and he kept tabs on what happened at school. He attended all of their soccer games and other activities and photographed or videotaped his children constantly. In 2011, Kim told *Redbook* magazine,

> My dad was the strict one, but he was still a lot of fun and always playing pranks. He believed that blood is thicker than water. That's how we always lived, with a total allegiance and loyalty to one another.[1]

Robert's grandparents had come to California from Armenia, and his Armenian heritage was important to him. He passed that love of his

ARMENIA

Armenia is a small country located in Western Asia. It is bordered by the countries of Turkey, Georgia, Azerbaijan, and Iran. Armenia is an independent nation ruled by a democratic government. In addition to the 3 million Armenians who live in the country, approximately 8 million more live around the world. Large Armenian populations can be found in Russia, Georgia, Iran, France, and the United States.

In Armenian culture, maintaining close relationships with family is important. Kim and her sisters frequently visited their Armenian grandparents on weekends, and the close-knit family often comes together over Armenian food. One of Kim's favorite Armenian foods is *Lamajune*, a traditional meal of round dough topped with spicy sauce and meat—Kim likes hers with string cheese. Kim Kardashian's last name gives away her ethnic identity. All Armenian names end in *ian*.

culture down to his children. The family lived near their Kardashian grandparents and often visited them. Kim later told an interviewer from *Armenian Pulse*, "We were raised with a huge Armenian influence, always hearing stories of Armenia, eating Armenian food, and celebrating Armenian holidays!"[2]

Kris was also a strong presence in the children's lives. She was the leader of the girls' Brownie troops, and she often volunteered in their classrooms and at school events. She encouraged her children to invite their friends over to the house so she could get to know everyone. Kris also taught her children strong values. She told *Redbook* magazine, "Our joy in life is that we always have each other. So I've tried to teach my kids

THE PEAK AND THE PIT

Kim and her sisters recalled one of their favorite dinnertime rituals. It was called the Peak and the Pit. Starting with Robert, the family would go around the table. Each member described the best part (the peak) and the worst part (the pit) of his or her day. This ritual brought the family closer together and kept everyone aware of what was going on in each other's lives.

three things: love God, love your family, and love yourself."[3]

||||||||||||||||||||||||||||||||||||||||||||||||||||

TROUBLES AND CHANGES

Even though the Kardashians were a tight, loving family, there was trouble in their house. In 1990, after 12 years of marriage, Robert and Kris divorced. Although the Kardashians have not revealed many details of Kris and Robert's marriage troubles, Kris initiated the divorce. She was not happy with the direction her life was going. Kim and her sisters didn't remember their parents fighting, so the news came as a surprise.

Kris and Robert told the children they were splitting up during a family meeting. Kim was ten years old at the time. Robert moved into another house that was not far from Tower Lane, and the girls and their brother visited him whenever they wanted. Robert also came to Tower Lane frequently, often eating dinner with his ex-wife and their children. The divorce was an amicable one, and Kris and Robert remained friendly, but the divorce was still upsetting, especially for the older girls.

Kim's family life got more complicated when her mother remarried in April 1991, not long after the divorce. Kim's stepfather was Bruce Jenner, an athlete and motivational speaker who became a national hero when he won a gold medal for the decathlon, a track and field event, at the 1976 Olympics. Bruce was also divorced, so Kim's family now included stepbrothers Burt, Brandon, and Brody and stepsister Casey. Kris and Bruce would later have two more children, Kendall and Kylie. Although Kim and Khloe liked Bruce from the start, Kourtney had a harder time adjusting to the new family arrangements and went to live with her father during high school. However, the two families eventually blended, and Robert and Bruce even became friends and golf partners.

At that time of her life, Kim was more concerned with her body than she was with her new stepfather. She had developed early and

EVERY BODY IS BEAUTIFUL ||||||||||||||||||||||||||||||||||||||||||||||||||||||

Though Kim struggled with body issues growing up, she came to love her curvy body and now often flaunts it in public. In *Kardashian Konfidential*, she encourages girls not to be ashamed of their bodies and to embrace themselves and their appearance, no matter what body shape they are.

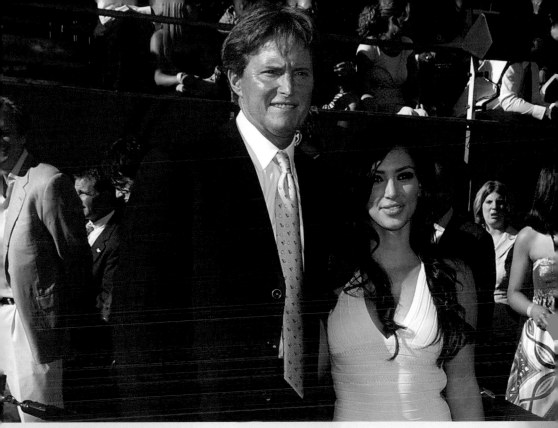

Kim has always had a good relationship with her stepfather, Bruce Jenner.

was often teased at school, which made her self-conscious about her curves. Kim wrote,

> I remember sitting in the bathtub during that time and crying, putting hot washcloths over my breasts to try to shrink them. I literally prayed to God, "Please don't let them grow any bigger!"[4]

Kim's mother reassured Kim she would someday learn to love her body.

MARYMOUNT HIGH SCHOOL CELEBRITIES

Kim was not the only celebrity who attended Marymount High School. Other celebrities include chef and Food Network star Giada De Laurentiis and actresses Mariska Hargitay and Marlo Thomas.

THE HIGH SCHOOL YEARS

In 1994, Kim began attending Marymount High School, an all-girls Catholic school in Bel Air, California. Although the family is not Catholic, Kim's parents liked the school's high academic standards and strict rules. Kim was a good student, was very involved in school clubs, and had an active social life. Because of the area where she lived, many of Kim's friends were from celebrity families. She briefly dated Michael Jackson's nephew and even attended a party at Neverland, Jackson's legendary ranch.

That year was also the start of another difficult time for Kim and her family. The Kardashians were good friends with O. J. Simpson, a former football player and actor, and his ex-wife, Nicole Brown Simpson. On June 12, 1994, Nicole and a friend were stabbed to death outside her home.

O. J. Simpson quickly became the prime suspect and was soon arrested for murder. The crime and the subsequent trial almost tore the Kardashians apart. Kris believed Simpson had murdered Nicole, who was one of Kris's best friends. Robert, on the other hand, became one of Simpson's lead defense attorneys. The trial captivated and outraged Americans. People followed and threatened Kim and her siblings because of their father's loyalty to Simpson. The children lost several friends because of the ordeal. Kim later called the period a very difficult time for her family and prefers not to talk about it in public.

Other than experiencing the O. J. Simpson trial firsthand, Kim's life was fairly typical of an upper-class California teen. There was one big difference,

THE O. J. SIMPSON TRIAL

The O. J. Simpson trial riveted America during 1994–1995. After Simpson, an African-American former football player, was acquitted of murdering his wife and her friend, both of whom were white, the trial exposed a racial divide in US society. Law expert Keith Wingate observed, "The Simpson trial has caused more ordinary Americans to look closely at the operation of our judicial system than any other event in recent memory. Moreover, the trial and the reactions to it say a great deal about our society as a whole and not just its legal system."[5]

however. Unlike most of her friends, Kim was not allowed to have a credit card. Although she and her sisters were allowed to shop and use their father's credit card to buy expensive designer clothes and shoes, they were expected to pay him back for every penny they spent. The Kardashians' parents also made it clear they would support the girls only while they were in school. Unless they went to college, they would be on their own once they graduated from high school. As Kim explained, "We may have been spoiled, but we weren't spoiled brats."[6]

Kim's father often made his daughters sign contracts about their behavior and what he expected them to do. When Kim was 16, her father bought her a car—and made her sign a two-page contract spelling out what expenses Kim would be responsible for, how she had to behave, and what grades she needed to achieve in order to keep the privilege of driving the car.

With her father's help, Kim started working when she was in high school. Robert owned a company called MovieTunes, which supplied the music played in theaters before a movie started. Kim worked for MovieTunes for several years.

Kim as a high school freshman in 1995

One of her jobs was burning CDs and sending them out to theaters all over the country. Kim enjoyed working for her father. She learned to be professional while at work, rather than taking advantage of her position as the boss's daughter. Her time at MovieTunes would be good training for her future business ventures.

||||||||||

Kardashian's mother, Kris, has acted as her manager from the start of Kardashian's career.

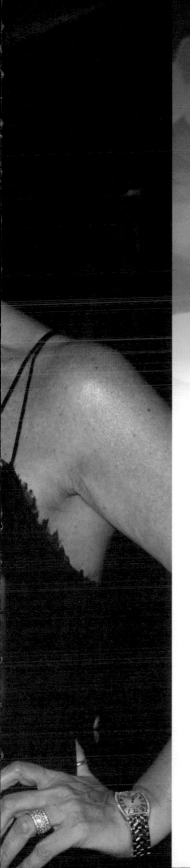

CHAPTER 3

Stylist and Socialite

||||||||||||||||||||||||||||||||||||||||||||||||||||

Kardashian graduated from Marymount High School in 1998. She enrolled in college but did not finish, which meant she had to find a job because her parents refused to support her if she was no longer in school. In 2010, Kardashian told *Entertainment Weekly*,

> We grew up in a life of privilege in Beverly Hills, but my parents'

KARDASHIAN GRADUATES

Of the four Kardashian children, only Kourtney and Rob graduated from college. Kourtney attended Southern Methodist University in Dallas, Texas, but later transferred to the University of Arizona at Tucson, where she received a degree in theater arts. Rob graduated from the University of Southern California with a degree in business.

mentality was like, "Okay, at 18, you're going to get cut off. If you want to maintain this lifestyle, you'll have to work at it." I always felt like I was lazy if I wasn't working.[1]

A YOUNG BUSINESSWOMAN

Kardashian's first business was organizing closets. She got the idea from organizing her friends' closets when she went to their houses for sleepovers or just to hang out. Kardashian was always very organized and interested in style, so this job was a natural fit for her.

When she was 18 years old, Kardashian also began selling clothes and accessories on eBay. Kardashian described herself as a "shopaholic," and she often bought things and later got tired of them. She found that selling these items on eBay was fun and profitable. It wasn't long before Kardashian was selling her friends' unwanted items as well. She would clean out and organize someone's closet and then sell the unwanted items, netting a share of the profit for herself.

Kardashian's interest in fashion helped guide her to her next career. When she was in her early twenties, she became a stylist. Her first client was her mother. At the time, Kris was doing television infomercials, and Kardashian thought the outfits she wore were not flattering. She asked her mother to let her find clothes for her to wear, and Kris agreed. "I just found it so easy," Kardashian wrote. "Mom looked great, so the company hired me to do other infomercials."[2] This success would eventually

LEARNING ON THE JOB

Although there are several schools and technical programs that offer degrees in fashion design, there are no specific classes for stylists. This is one career where natural talent and experience can lead to success. Kardashian did not learn how to be a stylist by going to school. Like most other stylists, she used her natural instincts and learned on the job. She also got tips from more experienced stylists.

WHAT IS A STYLIST?

Stylists are sometimes called wardrobe stylists or fashion stylists. A stylist selects the clothing for print or television advertising campaigns, magazine ads, photo shoots, music videos, and other public appearances. Stylists are usually part of a creative team that can include fashion designers, photographers, camera operators, hair and makeup artists, video or magazine art directors, and editors. The team works together to create a specific look for the project or campaign.

A stylist can have many different job responsibilities. Entry-level stylists may gather samples or items of clothing and bring them to more experienced stylists for consideration. More experienced stylists may work directly with designers to create or provide custom clothing for an event or promotional appearance. Some stylists work exclusively with a celebrity client to create their wardrobe, recommend outfits for public appearances, and do their personal shopping. Kardashian's responsibilities generally included choosing outfits for photo shoots and for public appearances by her clients. Like other stylists, Kardashian's goal was to choose clothes that flattered her clients' figures and made them look their best.

lead to her becoming a stylist and personal shopper for celebrities such as singer Brandy and actress Lindsey Lohan. She also used the tricks she'd learned to improve her own wardrobe and make the most of her physical features.

||||||||||||||||||||||||||||||||||||||||||||||||||||||

GETTING PERSONAL

Kardashian's personal life after high school was exciting as well. She had grown up and gone to school with many celebrities and stayed friends with them after graduation. Two of her best friends were Paris Hilton, part of the family that started the Hilton Hotel chain, and Nicole Richie, the daughter of musician Lionel Richie. Kardashian often accompanied her friends to nightclubs and parties. Soon her picture started appearing in magazines and tabloids. The public began to wonder who this dark-haired, curvy beauty was.

In 2000, 19-year-old Kardashian began dating music producer Damon Thomas, who was ten years older than her. One night, the two went to Las Vegas, Nevada, and got married. Kardashian kept her marriage a secret from her family, but it didn't take long for them to find out. After hearing rumors of the marriage from friends, Kourtney went online and found the couple's marriage license. Kourtney quickly shared the news with their mother. Kim was so angry Kourtney spilled her secret she didn't speak to her sister for several months. Finally, Robert insisted his daughters make up.

IIIIIIIIII

Kardashian was often sighted with her famous friend Paris Hilton.

Robert Kardashian taught his daughters business sense and the importance of family.

CHAPTER 4

Hard Times and Success

||||||||||||||||||||||||||||||||||||||||||||||||||||||||||||||||||||||||||

y 2003, Kardashian's marriage to Thomas was in trouble. Then she received another devastating blow. Her father became ill with esophageal cancer. On September 30, 2003, just eight weeks after he was diagnosed, Robert died. Kardashian and her siblings were devastated by his death. Kardashian wrote a speech and read it at his funeral. Along with her sisters, Kardashian

Many people believe Robert Kardashian left a lot of money to his children when he died. However, Robert remarried just six weeks before his death, and almost all his money and assets went to his new wife, rather than his children.

valued the lessons her father had taught the family, especially a love for their heritage, strong family ties, a powerful work ethic, and a good sense of humor.

MOVING ON

Her father's death helped Kardashian realize life was too short to remain in a situation that made her unhappy. She made the decision to divorce her husband. Kardashian's mother was not surprised the marriage did not work out. She later told *Redbook* magazine,

> *Kim didn't feel comfortable telling any of us because the situation wasn't meant to be. At the end of the day, you know you're not with the right person if he takes you to Vegas, marries you, and tells you not to tell your parents.*[1]

Kardashian filed for divorce from Thomas in 2004. She claimed her husband had hit and abused her. Thomas denied the claims, and the issue was never proven. A little older and much wiser, Kardashian knew it was time to move on with her life.

After her father's death, Kardashian continued working and socializing. In 2006, she and sisters, Kourtney and Khloe, opened a clothing store called Dash. The store was located in Calabasas. Each sister had a different job. Along with choosing the clothes, Kardashian helped customers by working

A FAMILY TRADITION

Owning a clothing store ran in the Kardashian family. For many years, Kim's grandmother owned a children's clothing store in La Jolla, California, near San Diego. Kim had fond memories of her mother taking the girls shopping at the store and buying them fashionable outfits, even when they were very young.

In 2003, Kourtney and her mother opened the children's clothing store Smooch in Calabasas. Opening Dash seemed like a natural next step. At first, only Kourtney and Khloe were going to open Dash. They didn't think Kim would be interested. When Kim found out, she was very upset and told her sisters she wanted to be involved. So Dash became a project all the sisters shared.

Kardashian put her sense of style to good use
when she and her sisters opened Dash.

as a personal shopper. She enjoyed choosing the
most flattering styles for her customers.

||||||||||||||||||||||||||||||||||||||||||||||||||

MORE RELATIONSHIPS

Around this time following her divorce, Kardashian became involved with a series of boyfriends. Kardashian later admitted to being insecure and letting people, including her boyfriends, treat her disrespectfully. She wrote of this period:

> I would date anyone who would give me attention. . . . I used to think maybe I didn't attract the right kind of people because I didn't look the way they wanted me to. I hadn't figured out yet that the real reason I wasn't attracting the right kind of person was because . . . I wasn't putting out my own sense of self-worth.[2]

One of Kardashian's more unfortunate relationships was with rapper Ray J. The two dated for a short time in 2007, but during that time, they made a tape containing sensitive content Kardashian wished to keep private. Although Kardashian swore she would never allow something so personal to fall into the hands of strangers, someone leaked the tape to the company Vivid Entertainment. Soon clips of the tape were available on the Internet. Then Vivid Entertainment began marketing the tape for sale.

Kardashian is interviewed on MTV in 2007,
several months after the scandal.

Kardashian was embarrassed and furious. She
sued Vivid to get back the rights to the tape and
eventually settled for a payment of $5 million. The
tape put Kardashian even more in the public eye;
she had caught the attention of the paparazzi and
the public in general.

LIFE IN THE SPOTLIGHT

In 2007, Kardashian and her family met with Ryan Seacrest, who had a production deal with E!, to discuss a possible reality show for the family. At

FACING EMBARRASSMENT

There was a frenzy of media attention when Kardashian's private tape was released. Many news sources compared Kardashian to other celebrities who had similar tapes released, including Pamela Anderson and Kardashian's friend Paris Hilton. It didn't help that Kardashian's partner on the tape, Ray J, was quoted saying the tape had been great for Kardashian's career and he was stunned she was upset at its release.

The public also had a strong reaction to the tape, especially after Kardashian became better known. Many people disliked Kardashian because of the tape and viewed her as having no talent, despite her business and entrepreneurial success. To these people, Kardashian was famous for only one thing.

Although Kardashian denied the tape's existence at first, she had no choice but to admit the truth when the video was released to the public. Since then, Kardashian has stated she is not proud of the tape and has attempted to move past the incident. In 2010, Kardashian told *Allure* magazine doing the tape was "not my [proudest] moment. It was humiliating. But now let's move on. Not that I don't think it's no one's business, but I think I've done a good job of replacing negative things with positive things."[3]

first, Seacrest and the executives at E! wondered if people would watch a show about a woman who was essentially famous only because of a scandal. Seacrest told an interviewer,

> *Frankly, at first I wondered if it [the tape] was going to be negative. I remember thinking [the situation] through—the upside, the downside—and I just felt like she was a great girl, she's a very hard worker, and I loved the dynamic she had with the family.*[4]

Keeping Up with the Kardashians began filming just a few weeks after the family met with him.

It took Kardashian and her sisters some time to get used to having their lives filmed, but they soon began enjoying the experience. The show sometimes included embarrassing moments and arguments between the family members, but it

NO SHAME ||||||||||||||||||||||||||||||||||||||||||||||||||||||||||||||||||||||||||||||||||||||||||||||

Kardashian told interviewers she doesn't mind having her life on display for everyone to see. She said, "There's nothing I'm really ashamed of, and I work hard on the show and all my other projects. I don't drink or do drugs, so I'm comfortable showing the world what my life is all about."[5]

Ryan Seacrest produced *Keeping Up with the Kardashians.*

always ended with apologies and plenty of love and affection. As Kardashian's stepfather, Jenner, told *Entertainment Weekly*, "When we originally talked about doing this, I told them that yes, we have drama, but the bottom line is that we all love each other. . . . It's about a family."[6]

Kardashian's mother, Kris, thought a television show would be a great way to get publicity and give Kardashian a less scandalous way to be famous. In addition, she saw the television show as a chance for family bonding. "We were still reeling . . . from the death of my ex-husband, and this opportunity was something for us to do together. It's a very safe feeling."[8]

In December, just months after *Keeping Up with the Kardashians* began filming, 27-year-old Kardashian was asked to pose nude for *Playboy* magazine. Her decision to do so became part of the show's storyline. For Kardashian, it was a hard choice. She was shy and not eager to show off her body in a magazine. She also knew her father would have hated the idea. However, her mother encouraged Kardashian to pose, and Kardashian felt it would be a good way to show her acceptance of her body. In the end, she said yes. "I knew Dad wouldn't approve, but I thought, 'I'm an adult now and I'm allowed to make the choice,'" Kardashian later wrote. "So I finally said yes. It was such a great experience. . . . I'm glad we showed me overcoming my fears on the show."[7] Several years later, however, in 2010, Kardashian told an interviewer from *Harper's Bazaar* she was sorry she had posed for *Playboy* and only did so because her mother made it sound like a positive experience.

The television show and resulting publicity made Kardashian and her family even more famous than the Simpson trial or tape had. At first, Kardashian found it hard to get used to her new fame. She was especially annoyed by tabloid rumors that she and her sisters were fighting or were jealous of each other. However, she and her family soon learned to laugh at the rumors and live their lives the way they wanted. Kardashian's attitude would come in handy during the years ahead.

DIRTY LAUNDRY

Executives at E! believed the Kardashians' willingness to be honest and open was the biggest reason for their show's success. Ted Harbert, president and CEO of E!'s parent company, Comcast Entertainment Group, complained about other reality stars whose shows failed because they were not willing to show their darker sides. He praised the Kardashians for knowing what viewers want to see. "The one thing reality viewers smell in an instant is if you're trying to hide or manipulate your image. The Kardashians decided early on: 'Hey, if we're going to do this, we're going to put it out there.'"[9]

Kardashian models for fashion designer Christian Audigier during a fashion show in 2007.

CHAPTER 5

At Work

||||||||||||||||||||||||||||||||||||||||||||||||||||||||||

Keeping Up with the Kardashians became an instant hit, and Kardashian and her family were becoming household names. Kardashian's increasing fame led to many more opportunities.

One of the new opportunities Kardashian encountered came in 2008 when she was invited to compete on the seventh season of the popular television show Dancing with the Stars. Kardashian's partner was professional ballroom dancer

Mark Ballas. The two got along well, but it turned out dancing was not one of Kardashian's talents. She was voted off the show during the third week of competition, finishing in eleventh place out of 13 participants. Kardashian said in a later episode of *Keeping Up with the Kardashians* she did not enjoy dancing or being away from her family and

DANCING WITH THE STARS

Dancing with the Stars premiered on American television in the summer of 2005. It is a spinoff of a British series called *Strictly Come Dancing*. The show pairs celebrities such as singers, athletes, models, and media personalities with professional ballroom dancers. Each week, the couples perform a predetermined dance routine from a dance style, such as a waltz or a tango. A panel of professional dancers judges the performances. Then viewers watching on television at home vote for their favorite couple by telephone. In the next episode, the following night, the results are announced and the couple with the lowest score goes home. The last remaining couple wins a mirror-ball trophy and a large cash prize. Past winners included actresses Kelly Monaco and Jennifer Grey, Olympic athletes Kristi Yamaguchi and Apolo Anton Ohno, and performers Donny Osmond and Nicole Scherzinger. The show is extremely popular and airs two seasons every year. Kim was the first member of the Kardashian clan to appear on the show, but her brother, Rob, appeared on the show during its thirteenth season in 2011.

Kardashian, with partner Mark Ballas, appeared on *Dancing with the Stars* in 2008.

was actually glad when she was voted off and sent home in October.

ACTRESS, MODEL, AND SPOKESPERSON

Kardashian also took some acting jobs during 2008. Her first appearance on the big screen was in the comedy spoof *Disaster Movie*. Kardashian had a supporting role. Although the movie was successful and Kardashian had fun filming it, no one was very impressed with her acting ability. In 2009, Kardashian had a small part in the movie *Deep in the Valley*. She also appeared on episodes of the television shows *CSI: NY* and *How I Met Your Mother* in 2009. In 2010, she played herself in the season premiere of the television series *90210*. Kardashian also appeared in several commercials, including a provocative ad for the fast-food chain Carl's Jr.

During the same time period, Kardashian had also started a thriving career as a model and spokesperson. In 2008, she began modeling for Bongo Jeans and Travis Barker's Famous Stars and Straps clothing line. She also modeled for Balenciaga shoes and was a model and spokesperson for Perfect Skin skin care products and QuickTrim weight loss products.

Some of Kardashian's endorsements led to legal problems. In 2009, she was involved with a lawsuit with Dr. Sanford Siegal, the creator of a diet program known as the Cookie Diet. Siegal posted an article on his Web site naming Kardashian as a celebrity who had seen positive results from the

Cookie Diet. Kardashian, who was under contract with QuickTrim at the time, put a message on her Twitter account saying Siegal was lying and she would never go on "this unhealthy diet."[1] She also sent a letter to Siegal demanding he remove any reference to her from his Web site. Siegal then sued Kardashian for defaming him. In February 2011, the lawsuit was dismissed.

||||||||||||||||||||||||||||||||||||||||||||||||||||||

A FASHIONABLE ENTREPRENEUR

Kardashian also became an entrepreneur, starting a line of her own products. In 2009, Kardashian became the cofounder and chief fashion stylist for ShoeDazzle, a shopping Web site for women's shoes. Along with her sisters, she also created two clothing lines for the clothing brands Bebe and

THE BRAINY KARDASHIAN? ||||||||||||||||||||||||||||||||||||||||||||

Kardashian, who is often known more for her body than her brain, has a sense of humor about her image. This was evident in a 2010 commercial to encourage tourism to her home state of California. In the commercial, Kardashian talks about common misconceptions about California while reading a heavy textbook about quantum physics.

Kardashian and her sisters designed a line of jewelry to be sold by Bebe.

Kardashian received an unusual honor in 2010. On July 1, Madame Tussauds Museum in New York City unveiled a wax figure of Kardashian wearing a revealing pink dress.

QVC. The clothes for Bebe, an upscale clothing store, were similar to items Kardashian would wear herself. The collection featured wrap dresses, off-the-shoulder gowns, jumpsuits in combinations of black and bright colors, and chunky accessories— all items were designed to show off the body and make the wearer feel glamorous. QVC, which sells numerous items on its television station, featured the K-Dash collection, with colorful dresses, tops, jackets, and pants.

Kardashian also released a series of workout DVDs called *Fit In Your Jeans By Friday*. And in February 2010, Kardashian released her own perfume, Kim Kardashian. The fragrance had a strong floral scent meant to invoke Kardashian's sultry style. Kardashian also teamed up with Kourtney and Khloe to create a line of Armenian-themed jewelry for the company Virgins, Saints, and Angels. The sisters also came up with a sunless

KARDASHIAN'S FRAGRANCE

Creating a fragrance is a painstaking process. Designers met with Kardashian and got a feeling for her personality, her likes and dislikes, and the type of scent she wore herself. Then they mixed chemicals to create an appealing scent that would remind people of Kardashian. Kardashian was involved in the fragrance's creation, testing scents and giving her opinion on what worked and what didn't. The result was a fragrance that combined floral scents, such as gardenia, tuberose, and white jasmine to evoke Kardashian's femininity with musky scents, such as sandalwood, Tonka bean, and jacaranda wood to create a warm, soft feeling that reflected Kardashian's presence. The bottle was also carefully designed to reflect Kardashian's bright, fun style. It featured pink and black colors and a large *KK* engraved into the side created a classic and stylish look.

tanner called Kardashian Glamour Tan, which is sold at Sephora, a cosmetics store.

Kardashian is proud of her business sense and believes *Keeping Up with the Kardashians* helped associate her and her brands with fashion and glamour. She told *Forbes* she's been a businesswoman since the days of working with her father and the television show "is definitely

Kardashian launched her fragrance, named after herself, in 2010.

our mothership and it's where we have created the
awareness of the Kardashian family."[2]

||||||||||

Kardashian ensured the success of her businesses by taking an active role in promotion. In 2010, she appeared at the opening of a new Dash store in New York.

CHAPTER 6

The Kardashian Empire

||||||||||||||||||||||||||||||||||||||||||

Kardashian and her sisters have said, "Being a celebrity is fun, but it doesn't pay the bills. . . . We're businesswomen to the core."[1] Kim proved this with the incredible array of business ventures she put together in the few years after *Keeping Up with the Kardashians* first went on the air.

Keeping Up with the Kardashians was still going strong in 2010 and 2011.

The E! network also launched three spinoff shows: *Kourtney and Khloe Take Miami*, *Khloe and Lamar*, and *Kourtney and Kim Take New York*. However, Kardashian had plenty to do besides filming her television shows. She and Kourtney were very much involved in the day-to-day work of running a new branch of Dash opened in New York City in 2010.

THE KARDASHIANS TAKE REALITY TV

Kourtney and Khloe Take Miami was launched in 2009 and followed Kourtney and Khloe as they opened a new branch of Dash in Miami, Florida. The focus of the show was on Kourtney's relationship with her boyfriend and Khloe's job at a Miami radio station. In 2010, Kourtney and Khloe turned over the day-to-day management of the Miami store to others. That fall, Kim appeared as part of a challenge on the reality show *The Apprentice* and as a guest judge on *America's Next Top Model*.

In 2011, Khloe returned to Los Angeles and launched another television show, *Khloe and Lamar*, which followed the lives of her and new husband, NBA player Lamar Odom. The same year, Kourtney moved to New York, where she had opened a branch of Dash with Kim in November 2010. She and Kim launched another reality show, *Kourtney and Kim Take New York*, in January 2011. Both sisters continued to star on *Keeping Up with the Kardashians*. Kim was also a guest judge on the reality fashion design show *Project Runway*.

Kardashian also made many personal appearances. She was paid thousands of dollars to appear in clubs and at parties all over the United States. Kardashian viewed these appearances not only as a good way to earn money, but also as a way to meet her fans and spread the news of her latest projects beyond the most media-covered cities, such as New York, Los Angeles, and Las Vegas.

Kardashian also was paid top dollar to model and appeared on several magazine covers after her rise to fame. Some of these magazines included US and international editions of *Redbook, People, W, Playboy*, and *FHM*.

||||||||||||||||||||||||||||||||||||||||||||||||||||

STUMBLING BLOCKS

Along with her successes, Kardashian faced a few obstacles in 2010 and 2011. In 2010, she tried her hand at producing, following in the footsteps of her friend Seacrest. She became the producer of a new reality show on E! called *The Spin Crowd*. The show focuses on six people who work at a Hollywood public relations firm and who are friends of Kardashian's. The show premiered on E!

on August 22. However, the show's ratings were not impressive. The finale aired less than two months later, on October 10, and E! did not renew the show.

Kardashian also attempted being a musician, but that effort failed too. In December 2010, she filmed a music video for a song she recorded called "Jam (Turn It Up)." Kardashian said she was encouraged to record the song by her friends in the music business, including the song's producer, rapper The-Dream. The song and video are featured on *Kourtney and Kim Take New York*, but Kardashian said she had no plans to record any other songs or videos or go any further with her music career. That was probably a good thing since the song was widely criticized. Critic Jim Farber wrote in the *Daily News* that the song was a "dead-

STAYING CLOSE TO HER FANS

Kardashian knows part of being a good businesswoman is being good to her fans. She keeps her thousands of fans updated on Twitter and generally doesn't mind meeting them and signing autographs, a task many celebrities find annoying. "I like to go out in the crowd and take pics," she said. "I like being myself. I don't want to be unapproachable."[2]

brained piece of generic dance music, without a single distinguishing feature" and called Kardashian "the worst singer in the reality TV universe."[3]

||||||||||||||||||||||||||||||||||||||||||||||||||||

SUCCESSES

Despite Kardashian's misadventures in producing and music, she tried and succeeded at other new things. In 2010, Saint Martin's Press published *Kardashian Konfidential*, a collection of stories, tips, and autobiographical information written by Kim, Kourtney, and Khloe. The book became a best seller, moving to number four on the *New York Times* Best Seller List just one week after its release. The book combines details about the Kardashian sisters' childhood and events in their adult lives. It also delves deeply into some personal topics, such as Kim's poor self-image when she was a teenager and the girls' reactions to their father's death. The book includes gossipy facts about the sisters as well as advice from them on being confident, true to yourself, and unafraid to take risks.

In another collaboration, the sisters were developing the Kardashian Kollection, a new clothing line that launched at Sears department stores in August 2011. The collection started with 41 clothing pieces, including curve-hugging dresses, jumpsuits, and underwear, along with accessories such as handbags, shoes, and jewelry. The clothes and accessories were all reasonably priced, and they were styled just like the clothes the Kardashian sisters wore. Kardashian was excited about the collection, calling it a way to "cater to our fans and make sure that everyone can have access to the Kardashian Kollection."[4]

In addition to designing, Kardashian also continued to model, make appearances, and create new perfumes. She even cowrote the novel *Dollhouse* with her sisters, which tells the juicy story of a trio of celebrity siblings with details based on the Kardashians' lives.

||||||||||||||||||||||||||||||||||||||||||||||||

DOWN TO BUSINESS

Kardashian was proud of how many businesses she had. She and her sisters believed they should be fully involved in their businesses and only took on projects they cared about. "We certainly don't jump at everything we're offered. No way," the sisters wrote in *Kardashian Konfidential*. "If we're going to

Khloe, Kourtney, and Kim's Kardashian Kollection consisted of clothing similar to styles the sisters actually wear day to day.

be involved in something, we have to make sure it reflects our lifestyle and values. We have to truly believe in it."[5]

Kardashian's mother has served as manager for Kardashian and her sisters for several years. She gets annoyed when people claim the Kardashian sisters are famous for doing nothing. "They get up at five every day and work until they fall down," Kris told *People* magazine. "They have the most amazing work ethic."[6]

Kris Jenner manages the careers of her daughters, and the girls call her "Momager," a combination of "Mom" and "manager." In addition to Kim's, Kourtney's, and Khloe's businesses, Kris also manages the modeling careers of her younger children, Kylie and Kendall.

Kardashian was quick to defend herself against critics:

> *If people say, 'You guys aren't talented, why should you have all this success?' we just figure, well, if you don't think we're talented, that's okay, but at least we hope you see that we've worked hard to be successful. Not everyone is going to like us, and there are always going to be a few people who make an issue of it. You can't make everyone happy, you just have to try to make yourself happy.*[7]

Kardashian may indeed have become famous because she was beautiful and privileged and was not afraid of putting her body and her life on display for the public. However, Kardashian took that attention and worked tirelessly to create opportunities for herself and her family. One writer for *Entertainment Weekly* reported,

> *The sisters have no illusions—they know the white-hot spotlight will eventually dim if not fade completely. Which is why Kim, Kourtney, and Khloe see the show as a means to an end— building a fan base, which they'll nurture with both social media and their retail and fashion businesses.*[8]

Ryan Schinman, an executive in the entertainment industry, agreed and also gave credit to manager Kris Jenner and producer Ryan Seacrest. He said, "[Kardashian] is the brand and

KARDASHIAN AND SOCIAL MEDIA

Kardashian has embraced social media as a way to both connect with her fans and promote herself. She constantly updates her Twitter account with details about what she is doing and where she is going. This allows her fans to follow her adventures and also provides great publicity for Kardashian's television shows, public appearances, and business ventures. Social media also gives Kardashian an interesting way to do product endorsements and make even more money. The British newspaper *The Guardian* reported Kardashian receives payments of up to $10,000 from sponsors for each tweet she broadcasts about them.

the people behind her are the people that are making the business decisions. Part of it is luck, part of it is timing, and part of it is great business."[9] Kardashian's business ventures were on a roll, but she hadn't put her personal life on hold to pursue them. As Kim's businesses were expanding, things had been heating up in her love life as well.

||||||||||

Kardashian reportedly
earned more than $100,000
for personal appearances
alone in 2010.

Kardashian started dating
Reggie Bush in 2007.

CHAPTER 7

Looking for Love

||||||||||||||||||||||||||||||||||||||||||||||||||||||||||||||||||||||||||||||||||||||||||||||

Kardashian has described herself as "a hopeless romantic."[1] After her failed marriage and a series of destructive relationships, by 2010 she had finally settled into a stable relationship with Reggie Bush, an NFL star running back for the New Orleans Saints. Kardashian and Bush met at the Excellence in Sports Performance Yearly (ESPY) Awards, hosted by the sports television network ESPN. The two dated for two and a half years. Kardashian later told several reporters she expected to get married and was even cutting out wedding dress photos from magazines. Kardashian was at the Super Bowl to cheer on her boyfriend when the Saints won the NFL Super Bowl in February 2010.

||||||||||||||||||||||||||||||||||||||||||||||||||||

LOVE LOST

The couple broke up soon after Bush's Super Bowl triumph. Kardashian blamed the breakup on the strain of a long-distance relationship. "It's hard when he's playing during the season and I'm filming my show," she told *Cosmopolitan*.[2] Kardashian also confessed to *People* magazine, "Once we spent too much time apart and got comfortable that way, it really took a toll on the relationship."[3]

Soon after her relationship with Bush ended, Kardashian began dating another football player, Dallas Cowboys wide receiver Miles Austin. As seen on *Keeping Up with the Kardashians*, Kardashian even flew to Dallas to spend just 24 hours with her new boyfriend. However, the pressure of being on television doomed the relationship, which was over by September 2010. "Had we gotten to know each other when we weren't filming, it would have been easier," Kardashian confessed. "He was thrust into a world that he didn't really want to be in."[4]

"When you're in the public eye and you're in a relationship, it seems like everyone (and by *everyone*, we mean the media) wants to know exactly where it's going at all times. . . . Most people just have to worry about their mother meddling in their love life, but we've got all sorts of people sticking their noses in all the time. If they don't really know much of anything, they just make up stories, like saying that your boyfriend is cheating on you. If the trust in your relationship isn't strong, that can put doubt in your mind."[5]

—KARDASHIAN KONFIDENTIAL

Kardashian's love life continued to be a source of fascination for the tabloids and the public. Around Thanksgiving in 2010, she was photographed at a basketball game with model Gabriel Aubry, movie star Halle Berry's ex-boyfriend. Tabloids soon reported Aubry had gone to Kardashian's house for

Kardashian and her sisters knew the family's united front could sometimes scare away potential boyfriends. In *Kardashian Konfidential*, they wrote, "Date one of us, date us all. If you're a Kardashian, you simply cannot have a relationship without everyone in the whole family being part of it. . . . We're very protective of each other."[9]

Thanksgiving dinner. However, the couple only dated a few times and were never really serious.

In November 2010, Kardashian told *People* magazine, "I thought I would be married by now."[6] Still, she said while she was eager to fall in love and get married, she was no longer "desperately looking for it."[7] She added that she was happy to date and have fun and was in no rush to get married. "Give me a few years before that happens," she said. "A guy isn't the only thing that will make me happy."[8]

|||||||||||||||||||||||||||||||||||||||||||||||||||||||

LOVE FOUND

Given her comments in the *People* article, it surprised some people when Kardashian moved quickly into another serious relationship with yet another athlete. In December 2010, she began dating New Jersey Nets basketball player Kris Humphries. The relationship had its rocky moments, as chronicled on *Keeping Up with the Kardashians*. During a family trip to Bora Bora, Humphries annoyed other members of the Kardashian family with his boisterous actions and pranks, such as throwing Kardashian and her brother Rob into the ocean. Kardashian's sisters also distrusted Humphries and were not openly welcoming to him. In addition, Humphries sometimes seemed annoyed at Kardashian's privileged upbringing and clearly thought she sometimes acted like a spoiled princess. Still, the couple grew closer, and in May 2011, just six months after they started dating, Kardashian and Humphries got engaged.

QUICK COURTSHIPS

Kardashian wasn't the only member of her family to marry an NBA player after a short courtship. In September 2009, Khloe married basketball player Lamar Odom after they had only known each other for a month. That relationship was longer lived, however. The couple was still together at the time of Kardashian's divorce in 2011.

Some close to Kardashian questioned her and Humphries's decision to get engaged after dating only a few months.

AN EXTRAVAGANT WEDDING

Kardashian and Humphries wed on August 20, 2011. The event was one of the media sensations of the year. In the weeks before the wedding, Kardashian constantly updated her Web site and Twitter feeds, sharing details with her fans about her pre-wedding gym workouts, dress fittings, cake tastings, and other preparations. Magazines also published photos and details about the wedding, the rehearsal dinner, and all the preparations. One marketing expert said,

> People have shared her love story and everyone is so excited. Not everyone can be invited to her wedding, but she brings people in with her blog, [and] with a TV special on E! She genuinely wants to share the moment with her fans because she cares that much about them.[10]

Some people, however, were critical of Kardashian's wedding. The event was called a publicity stunt and led to many jokes about whether the marriage would be over by the time the E! special aired two months later. Kardashian did her best to ignore their comments.

The wedding itself took place at an estate in a seaside canyon in the town of Montecito, California. During the ceremony and the reception, Kardashian wore three different gowns, all designed by famous dress designer Vera Wang. The traditional Christian ceremony included touches that were over-the-top Kardashian, including a huge cross bedazzled with crystals. "It was so

EMOTIONAL MOMENTS ||||||||||||||||||||||||||||||||||||||||||||||||||||||||||||||||||

The E! television special, *Kim's Fairy Tale Wedding: A Kardashian Event*, revealed that Kardashian and her fiancée, Kris Humphries, were under a lot of stress in the weeks leading up to the wedding. Kardashian's vision of the wedding was a lot more elaborate than Humphries's, and the two often clashed on the details. Kardashian also managed every aspect of the wedding, making Humphries feel she didn't value his opinion. Kardashian often became annoyed at Humphries's joking around and felt he wasn't taking the wedding seriously, while she felt it was the most important day of her life.

Just a few days before the wedding, Kardashian revealed a deeper source of anxiety. She desperately missed her late father and wished he could be there to see her special day. As a way of honoring and remembering her father, Kardashian had some of his clothes taken out of storage and chose a shirt she remembered him wearing frequently. From the shirt, Kardashian cut out three heart-shaped pieces and had one sewn into each of the three wedding dresses she wore.

Kardashian and Humphries's extravagant wedding was seen by some as a publicity stunt.

hard to take it all seriously," said a guest who was amused at all the glitter and the overwhelming details of the ceremony and decorations.[11] All the camera crews and network technicians who were on hand to film the wedding also bothered the guests. Even Kardashian admitted, "It was over-the-top glam but just so elegant."[12]

The wedding was estimated to cost millions of dollars, including the cost of the diamonds Kardashian wore. However, media reports stated the Kardashians didn't have to pay for any of it. Many of the wedding details were given to Kardashian for free in exchange for publicity, including her hair and makeup preparations, the cake, the invitations, and the three dresses. Kardashian even managed to make money on the affair, selling photo rights to *People* magazine for $1.5 million. E! expected to earn approximately $15 million from the *Kim's Fairy Tale Wedding: A Kardashian Event* special. That money will be split between the Kardashians, producer Ryan Seacrest, and E!

After the wedding, Kardashian and Humphries jetted off to Italy for a short honeymoon. It wasn't long before Kardashian was back in the United States and ready for work.

THE FAIRY TALE ENDS

Kardashian may have had her fairy-tale wedding, but it did not take long before cracks began to appear in her marriage. Unlike most couples,

Kardashian and Humphries appeared on *The Tonight Show with Jay Leno* to discuss married life just weeks before Kardashian filed for divorce.

who are able to settle down into their own home and create a new life together, the early days of Kardashian and Humphries's marriage were filled with uncertainty. Humphries was unable to play professional basketball because the NBA had locked out its players and postponed the basketball season during a labor dispute between players and owners. Humphries was not even sure what team he would be playing for when the lockout ended, which meant he didn't know what city his home base would be. Work-driven Kardashian soon claimed to be annoyed at Humphries's lack of ambition and purpose.

The couple would be filming episodes of the TV show *Kourtney and Kim Take New York*, so they settled in New York City for the time being. Instead of getting a place of their own, they moved into a hotel suite with Kourtney, her boyfriend, Scott Disick, and their two-year-old son, Mason. Living with other family members was stressful and did not allow the newlyweds to really get to know each other.

Within weeks of the wedding, tabloids were buzzing with rumors of trouble in the marriage. The couple did not spend a lot of time together and seemed uncomfortable during public appearances. When Kardashian jetted off to the Arab country of Dubai for a four-day business trip, she was accompanied, not by Humphries, but by her mother. During her absence, stories circulated of Humphries partying and flirting with other girls back in New York.

Finally, on October 31, 2011, just 72 days after their lavish wedding, Kardashian filed for divorce.

In a statement to the press, she said, "I hope that everyone understands that this was not an easy decision. I had hoped this marriage was forever, but sometimes things don't work out as planned."[13]

Many people accused Kardashian of faking the marriage for publicity and a storyline for her TV show, but Kardashian herself and sources close to the family denied this. They described Kardashian as a romantic who got caught up in a dream come true moment.

"Everyone that knows me knows that I'm a hopeless romantic! I love with all of my heart and soul. I want a family and babies and a real life so badly that maybe I rushed in to something too soon. I believed in love and the dream of what I wanted so badly. I felt like I was on a fast roller coaster and couldn't get off when now I know I probably should have. I got caught up with the hoopla and the filming of the TV show that when I probably should have ended my relationship, I didn't know how to and didn't want to disappoint a lot of people."[14]

—KIM KARDASHIAN DISCUSSING HER DIVORCE ON HER BLOG

Rumors started flying when Kardashian left her new husband at home and took her mother along on a trip to Dubai in October.

It seemed as soon as the romance of the wedding and honeymoon wore off, it became clear Kardashian and Humphries really did not know each other at all. They had such different values, backgrounds, and goals that some said the marriage had been doomed to fail. But Kardashian never stayed down for long, and she had plenty of other endeavors to keep her mind off her failed second marriage.

||||||||||||

Kardashian has used her fame to help many charities and causes.

City of
Hope.™

ity of
ope.™

CHAPTER 8

Giving Back and Looking Forward

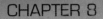

Kardashian earned more than $6 million in 2010, making her the highest paid reality television star. Although Kardashian lives an extravagant life, she credits her father with teaching her to give back. During a 2011 appearance on the CNN talk show *Piers Morgan's Tonight*, she told Morgan she donates 10 percent of her income to charity. Most of the money goes to a church in Calabasas as well as to The Dream Foundation, a charity that grants wishes for terminally ill adults. The foundation approached Kardashian and her sisters to grant wishes, and the sisters liked the charity's work, so Kardashian decided to give the organization even more support. She said of her charity work,

> It's not just about giving away, it's about finding something you really connect with. So many people ask us to donate money, [but] some things just don't make sense to me and I don't feel connected or passionate to that certain thing. So when I find something I like, like The Dream Foundation, it makes it just so much more meaningful.[1]

THE DREAM FOUNDATION ||||||||||||||||||||||||||||||||||||||||||||||||||||||||||||||||

The Dream Foundation is a charity that grants wishes for terminally ill adults. Thomas Rollerson founded the organization in 1993. Rollerson was aware of charities such as the Make A Wish Foundation and the Starlight Foundation that granted wishes to seriously ill children, and he was surprised to find out that there was no organization like that for adults. The Dream Foundation's goal is to make dreams come true for people who are not expected to survive for more than a year.

More than 1 million people died in the Armenian Genocide in the years before, during, and after World War I. Fortunately for the Kardashians, their ancestors had already left Armenia and settled in California before the genocide occurred.

After filing for divorce from Humphries, Kardashian donated the value of the wedding gifts the couple had received to The Dream Foundation.

||||||||||||||||||||||||||||||||||||||||||||||||||||||||

ACTIVISM AND PHILANTHROPY

Kardashian has used her fame to raise awareness for a variety of issues. As a fervent supporter of the Armenian community, Kardashian has spoken publicly urging recognition of the Armenian Genocide, a mass extermination campaign conducted in the Ottoman Empire (now part of eastern Europe, including Turkey) that killed more than 1 million Armenians between 1915 and 1923. Kardashian has mentioned the Armenian Genocide in media interviews, on her blog, and on Twitter.

Kardashian uses her celebrity to raise awareness for different causes and social issues.

She has also spoken out against the repressive political situation and government in Burma. Additionally, she has been a spokesperson for the Give a Damn Campaign, which aims to create awareness of discrimination against the lesbian, gay, bisexual, and transgender (LGBT) community.

Kardashian has also lent her fame to fund-raisers for other causes, including breast cancer and AIDS awareness. She knows the power of celebrity and uses it to draw attention to causes she believes in.

||||||||||||||||||||||||||||||||||||||||||||||||

KARDASHIAN: TO BE KONTINUED

Because she is so family oriented, Kardashian enjoys sharing her success with her entire family. Although Kim is the most famous of the Kardashians, she is happy to share the spotlight with Khloe, Kourtney, and the other members of her family. Kardashian and her sisters are intelligent businesswomen who have succeeded in most endeavors they have undertaken together.

Kardashian may have gotten attention for all the wrong reasons at first, but she has proven herself to be a pro at keeping the public interested in her, and she has turned that attention into good publicity and big money. Kardashian is more than just a pretty face—she is a brand. And although some may look down on Kardashian for the seemingly superficial things she represents, it's difficult not to admire her for her ambition, glamour, and success.

> "It's annoying when I hear, 'What do your girls do?' Well, first of all, all my daughters have jobs. They are fashion stylists and designers; they own a chain of stores. They had the stores before they had the show. And my kids worked from the time they were 13 years old. So to me, that's a huge misconception—that the girls don't work. They work 25 hours a day. And that they don't have any talent? They might not be singers or dancers, but they certainly know how to produce a television show."[2]
>
> —KRIS JENNER DEFENDING HER DAUGHTERS IN AN INTERVIEW WITH REDBOOK

Some people may not like Kardashian, but she has no intention of slowing down. With her second marriage and divorce behind her, she still has the support of her family. She believes she and her sisters still have a lot to achieve and the future will be bright. Kardashian also looks back to her past for inspiration, saying, "If my dad were alive today, I think he'd tell me that he is very proud of us! He

Through all her ups and downs, Kardashian has remained
a figure of fascination to the media and the public.

was very business-oriented and family was very
important. We represent everything he taught us."[3]

||||||||||

1980

1998

1998

On October 21, Kimberly Noel Kardashian is born in Los Angeles, California.

Kardashian graduates from Marymount High School in June.

Kardashian begins selling goods on eBay.

2006

2007

2007

Kardashian and her sisters open the first Dash boutique.

Kardashian dates rap singer Ray J. Vivid Entertainment leaks the couple's private tape onto the Internet.

Kardashian begins dating football star Reggie Bush.

2000

2003

2004

Kardashian secretly marries Damon Thomas in Las Vegas, Nevada.

Robert Kardashian dies of cancer on September 30.

Kardashian divorces Damon Thomas.

2007

2007

2008

In October, Kardashian and her family's reality show *Keeping Up with the Kardashians* premieres.

Kardashian poses for *Playboy* magazine in December.

Kardashian appears in *Disaster Movie*.

TIMELINE

2008

2008

2009

Kardashian appears on *Dancing with the Stars* but is voted off on the third episode.

Kardashian models for Bongo Jeans and Balenciaga shoes and appears as a model and spokesperson for Perfect Skin and QuickTrim.

Kardashian becomes the cofounder and chief fashion stylist for ShoeDazzle.

2010

2011

2011

Kardashian begins dating Kris Humphries in December.

In January, Kardashian stars in a second reality series, *Kourtney and Kim Take New York*.

Kardashian marries Humphries in a lavish ceremony in California on August 20.

2010

2010

2010

Kardashian's perfume debuts in February.

In November, Kardashian and her sister Kourtney open a branch of Dash in New York City.

The Kardashian sisters publish *Kardashian Konfidential*.

2011

2011

2011

The Kardashian Kollection debuts at Sears on August 24.

E! airs Kardashian's wedding as a special two-part television event in October.

On October 31, Kardashian files for divorce from Humphries.

FULL NAME

Kimberly Noel Kardashian

DATE OF BIRTH

October 21, 1980

PLACE OF BIRTH

Los Angeles, California

MARRIAGE

Damon Thomas (January 22, 2000)

Kris Humphries (August 20, 2011)

SELECTED FILMS AND TELEVISION APPEARANCES

Keeping Up with the Kardashians (2007–2011), *Disaster Movie* (2008), *Deep in the Valley* (2009), *Kourtney and Kim Take New York* (2011), *Kim's Fairytale Wedding: A Kardashian Event* (2011)

PUBLICATIONS

Kardashian Konfidential (2010), *Dollhouse* (2011)

BUSINESS

Kardashian co-owns Dash clothing boutiques in Calabasas, Miami, and New York City. She and her sisters have also designed clothing lines for QVC, Bebe, and Sears. Kardashian is cofounder and chief stylist of ShoeDazzle. She launched her own fragrance in 2010. Kardashian continues to expand her career through acting, modeling, and promoting various products.

PHILANTHROPY

Kardashian has actively supported the Dream Foundation, which grants wishes for terminally ill adults. She has also helped raise awareness about issues such as the Armenian Genocide, HIV/AIDS, breast cancer, and LGBT rights.

"If people say, 'You guys aren't talented, why should you have all this success?' we just figure, well, if you don't think we're talented, that's okay, but at least we hope you see that we've worked hard to be successful. Not everyone is going to like us, and there are always going to be a few people who make an issue of it. You can't make everyone happy, you just have to try to make yourself happy."

—KIM KARDASHIAN

amicable—Characterized by friendly goodwill.

asset—An item of value owned.

boutique—A small, fashionable shop.

entrepreneur—One who organizes, manages, and assumes the risks of a business.

infomercial—A television program that is an extended advertisement.

lavish—Marked by excess.

paparazzi—Aggressive photojournalists who take pictures of celebrities and sell them to media outlets.

personal shopper—Someone who chooses flattering clothing for clients and helps them dress and look their best.

philanthropy—An act of charity, such as a donation, for a humanitarian or environmental purpose.

premiere—The first public showing.

scandal—Loss of or damage to reputation caused by actual or apparent violation or morality or propriety.

spoof—A light, humorous, often ridiculous imitation of something.

tabloids—News organizations that focus on celebrities and celebrity gossip.

union—A group that protects the rights of workers in a particular occupation.

venture—An undertaking involving chance, risk or danger; a speculative business enterprise.

SELECTED BIBLIOGRAPHY

Berger, Lori. "Love, Kardashian Style." *Redbook* May 2011: 200–207. Print.

Garcia, Jennifer. "I'm Ready for Love." *People* 22 Nov. 2010: 68–71. Print.

Goodreau, Jenna. "Reality Stars Turned Entrepreneurs." *Forbes.com*. Forbes.com, 13 Apr. 2010. Web. 15 Sept. 2011.

Jensen, Jeff. "Naked Ambition: Why Are These Women Famous?" *Entertainment Weekly* 3 Sept. 2010: 42–46. Print.

Kardashian, Kourtney, Kim Kardashian, and Khloe Kardashian. *Kardashian Konfidential*. New York: St. Martin's, 2010. Print.

Malcolm, Shawna. "Up in Kim Kardashian's Business." *Cosmopolitan* Nov. 2009: 40–44. Print.

FURTHER READINGS

Brashich, Audrey D. *All Made Up: A Girl's Guide to Seeing Through Celebrity Hype and Celebrating Real Beauty*. New York: Walker, 2006. Print.

Edwards, Posy. *The Kardashians: A Krazy Life*. London: Orion, 2012. Print.

Senker, Cath. *Fashion Designers*. New York: PowerKids, 2012. Print.

WEB SITES

To learn more about Kim Kardashian, visit ABDO Publishing Company online at **www.abdopublishing.com**. Web sites about Kim Kardashian are featured on our Book Links page. These links are routinely monitored and updated to provide the most current information available.

PLACES TO VISIT

Dash Boutique
4774 Park Granada, Suite #5
Calabasas, CA 91302
818-222-4122
The Dash store in Calabasas, California, was the first of the line of clothing boutiques opened by Kim, Khloe, and Kourtney Kardashian.

Famous Cupcakes
4820 Laurel Canyon Boulevard
North Hollywood, CA 91607
1-888-774-9140
http://www.famouscupcakes.com
Try a Va-Va-Va-Nilla cupcake at Famous Cupcakes. The flavor was created for Kardashian.

Madame Tussauds Wax Museum
234 West 42nd Street
New York, NY 10036
866-841-3505
http://www.madametussauds.com/NewYork/Default.aspx
Kim Kardashian is immortalized in wax at Madame Tussauds Wax Museum in New York.

CHAPTER 1. TV'S NEWEST STAR

1. Kourtney, Kim, and Khloe Kardashian. *Kardashian Konfidential*. New York: St. Martin's Press, 2010. Print. 100.

2. Ibid. 102.

3. Moorfoot, Addie. "Ryan Seacrest." *Daily Variety* 15 Sept. 2009: A13. Print.

4. "Keeping Up with the Kardashians Season One." *PopMatters*. PopMatters.com, 16 Oct. 2008. Web. 15 Aug. 2011.

5. "Variety Reviews—Keeping Up with the Kardashians." *Variety*. RBI, 10 Oct. 2007. Web. 15 Aug. 2011.

CHAPTER 2. GROWING UP KARDASHIAN

1. Lori Berger. "Love, Kardashian Style!" *Redbook* May 2011: 206. Print.

2. Harout Kalandjian. "Kim Kardashian—The Armenian Interview." *Armenian Pulse*. Armenian Pulse Radio & Entertainment, 3 Apr. 2010. Web. 15 Sept. 2011.

3. Lori Berger. "Love, Kardashian Style!" *Redbook* May 2011: 202. Print.

4. Kourtney, Kim, and Khloe Kardashian. *Kardashian Konfidential*. New York: St. Martin's Press, 2010. Print. 31.

5. Keith Wingate. "The O.J. Simpson Trial: Seeing the Elephant." *UC Hastings College of the Law.* UC Hastings College of the Law, 2011. Web. 15 Aug. 2011.

6. Kourtney, Kim, and Khloe Kardashian. *Kardashian Konfidential*. New York: St. Martin's Press, 2010. Print. 40.

CHAPTER 3. STYLIST AND SOCIALITE

1. Jeff Jensen. "Naked Ambition: Why are These Women Famous?" *Entertainment Weekly* 3 Sept. 2010: 42–46. Print.

2. Kourtney, Kim, and Khloe Kardashian. *Kardashian Konfidential*. New York: St. Martin's Press, 2010. Print. 72.

CHAPTER 4. HARD TIMES AND SUCCESS

1. Lori Berger. "Love, Kardashian Style!" *Redbook* May 2011: 206. Print.

2. Kourtney, Kim, and Khloe Kardashian. *Kardashian Konfidential*. New York: St. Martin's Press, 2010. Print. 90 92.

3. "Kim Kardashian on Her Sex Tape: 'Not My Most Proud Moment.'" *In Case You Didn't Know*. In Case You Didn't Know, 17 Aug. 2010. Web. 8 Oct. 2011.

4. Jeff Jensen. "Naked Ambition: Why are These Women Famous?" *Entertainment Weekly* 3 Sept. 2010: 42–46. Print.

5. Lori Berger. "Love, Kardashian Style!" *Redbook* May 2011: 203. Print.

6. Jeff Jensen. "Naked Ambition: Why are These Women Famous?" *Entertainment Weekly* 3 Sept. 2010: 42 46. Print.

7. Kourtney, Kim, and Khloe Kardashian. *Kardashian Konfidential*. New York: St. Martin's Press, 2010. Print. 102.

8. Jeff Jensen. "Naked Ambition: Why are These Women Famous?" *Entertainment Weekly* 3 Sept. 2010: 42–46. Print.

9. Jeff Jensen. "Naked Ambition: Why are These Women Famous?" *Entertainment Weekly* 3 Sept. 2010: 42–46. Print.

CHAPTER 5. AT WORK

1. Gina DiNunno. "Kim Kardashian Sued by Cookie Diet Doc Over a Tweet." *TV Guide*. TV Guide, 6 Jan. 2010. Web. 24 Sept. 2011.

2. "Dash of Reality: Kim Kardashian." *Forbes.com*. Forbes.com, LLC, n.d. Web. 15 Sept. 2011.

CHAPTER 6. THE KARDASHIAN EMPIRE

1. Kourtney, Kim, and Khloe Kardashian. *Kardashian Konfidential*. New York: St. Martin's Press, 2010. Print. 213.

2. Marianne Garvey. "5 Things We Learned From Kardashian Konfidential." *Today Celebrities*. E! Entertainment Television, 29 Nov. 2010. Web. 27 Sept. 2011.

3. Jim Farber. "Kim Kardashian Song 'Jam (Turn It Up)' Makes Her the Worst Singer in the Reality TV Universe." *Daily News*. NYDailyNews.com, 2 Mar. 2011. Web. 20 Sept. 2011.

4. Rachel Brown. "Sears Looks to Kardashians to Amp Up Apparel." *Los Angeles Times*. Los Angeles Times, 12 Jan. 2011. Web. 12 Oct. 2011.

5. Kourtney, Kim, and Khloe Kardashian. *Kardashian Konfidential*. New York: St. Martin's Press, 2010. Print. 100.

6. "Kris Jenner: The Mom of Six is Relaxing—A Little!" *People* 15 Aug. 2011: 80. Print.

7. Kourtney, Kim, and Khloe Kardashian. *Kardashian Konfidential*. New York: St. Martin's Press, 2010. Print. 143.

8. Jeff Jensen. "Naked Ambition: Why are These Women Famous?" *Entertainment Weekly* 3 Sept. 2010: 42–46. Print.

9. Sandy Cohen. "Kim's Wedding is Big Business for the Kardashians." *Yahoo Finance*. Associated Press. 19 Aug. 2011. Web. 27 Aug. 2011.

CHAPTER 7. LOOKING FOR LOVE

1. Kourtney, Kim, and Khloe Kardashian. *Kardashian Konfidential*. New York: St. Martin's Press, 2010. Print. 192.

2. Shawna Malcolm. "Up in Kim Kardashian's Business." *Cosmopolitan* Nov. 2009: 40–44. Print.

3. Jennifer Garcia. "I'm Ready for Love." *People* 22 Nov. 2010: 68–71. Print.

4. Ibid.

5. Kourtney, Kim, and Khloe Kardashian. *Kardashian Konfidential*. New York: St. Martin's Press, 2010. Print. 200.

6. Jennifer Garcia. "I'm Ready for Love." *People* 22 Nov. 2010: 68–71. Print.

7. Ibid.

8. Ibid.

9. Kourtney, Kim, and Khloe Kardashian. *Kardashian Konfidential*. New York: St. Martin's Press, 2010. Print. 194.

10. Sandy Cohen. "Kim's Wedding is Big Business for the Kardashians." *Yahoo Finance*. Associated Press. 19 Aug. 2011. Web. 27 Aug. 2011.

11. Jennifer O'Neill. "Inside Kim's Lavish Wedding." *US Weekly* 5 Sept. 2011: 56. Print.

12. Jennifer Garcia. "Kim's Storybook Wedding." *People* 5 Sept. 2011: 76. Print.

13. Jennifer Garcia and Mike Fleeman. "Kim Kardashian: Why I Filed for Divorce from Kris Humphries. *People*. Time Inc., 31 Oct. 2011. Web. 2 Nov. 2011.

14. Kim Kardashian. "A Message to My Fans." *Kim Kardashian*. BUZZmedia Entertainment, 1 Nov. 2011. Web. 2 Nov. 2011.

CHAPTER 8. GIVING BACK AND LOOKING FORWARD

1. Marianne Garvey. "Give It Away Now: Kim Kardashian Says She Donates 10 Percent of Her Income to Charity." *E! Online*. E! Entertainment Television, 27 Jan. 2011. Web. 28 Sept. 2011.

2. Lori Berger. "Love, Kardashian Style!" *Redbook* May 2011: 202. Print.

3. Shawna Malcolm. "Up in Kim Kardashian's Business." *Cosmopolitan* Nov. 2009: 40–44. Print.

Joanne Mattern has been writing for children for many years. She is the author of more than 250 books for young readers and specializes in nonfiction. Her favorite topics include biographies, animals and nature, history, and sports. Joanne started her career as an editor and worked at several major publishers before becoming a full-time writer. She lives in New York State with her husband, children, and an assortment of pets.

PHOTO CREDITS

Denise Truscello/WireImage/PR Newswire/AP Images, cover, 3; Paul Drinkwater/NBCU Photo Bank/AP Images, 6; Michael Tran/FilmMagic/Getty Images, 10; Ethan Miller/ Getty Images, 15; E! Entertainment Television/Photofest, 16; Seth Poppel/Yearbook Library, 19, 20, 29, 97 (top); Luis Martinez/AP Images, 25; Jeff Vespa/WireImage/Getty Images, 30, 47; Tammie Arroyo/AP Images, 37; Kevan Brooks/ AdMedia/Shutterstock Images, 38; Chris Polk/FilmMagic/ Getty Images, 42, 96; Evan Agostini/AP Images, 44, 56, 72, 97 (bottom); Matt Sayles/AP Images, 50; ABC Inc/Everett/ Rex USA, 53; Ian West/PA Wire/AP Images, 59, 99 (top); Donald Traill/AP Images, 60; Harmony Gerber/Shutterstock Images, 67, 99 (bottom); Rena Schild/Shutterstock Images, 71, 100; Shutterstock Images, 78, 98; Albert Michael/ startraksphoto.com, 81; Paul Drinkwater/NBC/NBCU Photo Bank/AP Images, 83; JJC/Rex Features/AP Images, 86; John Sciulli/Getty Images, 88; Lev Radin/Shutterstock Images, 92; Andrew Toth/PatrickMcMullan.com/AP Images, 95